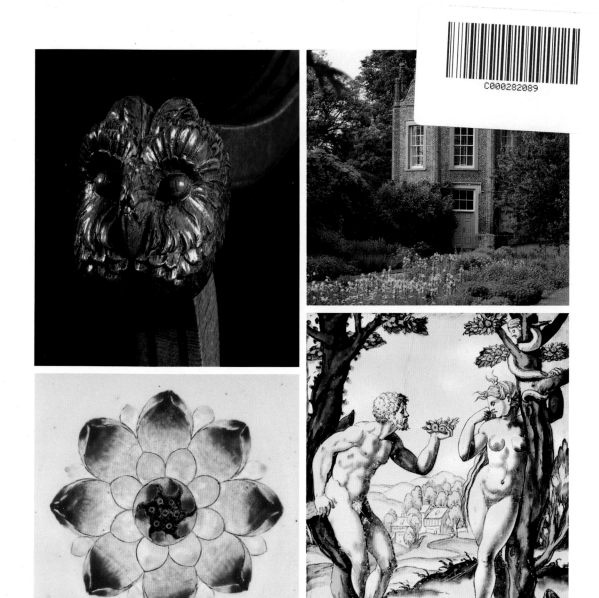

Melford Hall

Suffolk

Wartime memories of Melford Hall

by Sir Richard Hyde Parker, Bt

I was born at Melford Hall, followed by my sister two years later on the day war was declared. The house was then requisitioned and occupied by the army, and we moved to a house on the green opposite. My strongest early memories go back to 1942, when I was nearly five, watching the house burning in the distance. That afternoon I walked hand-in-hand with my father to the scene, which was comparable, at my age, to a burnt-out box on a bonfire. On the following day, my father marked the timber on the estate to be felled for rebuilding.

The fire gutted the north wing and destroyed adjoining roofs. Water from the firemen's hoses also caused extensive damage to important interiors and subsequently dry-rot. Prof. Sir Albert Richardson was the only architect prepared to restore the wing without demolishing the surviving structure, and his successful use of an internal concrete frame remains visible today. I remember him as a kindly old man, impressing us children by producing a miniature watercolour box from his pocket to illustrate his schemes.

I continued to grow up in a world where the trappings of war divorced from serious action were delight to a small boy living at the hub of military activity; when Wrigley's Spearmint and B-17 bombers made the greatest impression on boys of my age in the village.

Men from twelve successive battalions from nine regiments made the house and the Nissen huts in the park their home. Until, finally, in June 1944 the 1st Battalion of the Royal Hampshire Regiment was inspected by King

The north wing was completely gutted by the fire

George VI at Melford Hall before going into action as spearhead troops in the assault on Gold Beach during the D-Day landings.

My final memories of the war are as a child on VE Day, standing by the biggest bonfire I had ever seen, on Long Melford Green. There were no fireworks during the war, so the army fired endless flares that criss-crossed the sky like searchlights, but in red, green and yellow. The concept of victory made less impression then than the diversity of the gathering lit by the flames. There were troops from the camps at Melford Hall and Kentwell Hall, Americans from the aerodromes at Alpheton and Acton, and us from Melford with the many evacuees who came from London to live with us. And yet victory was to herald loss of freedom for future generations of

(Left) Sir Richard Hyde Parker with his father on the bowling green at Melford Hall about 1940

(Right) The Cordell Room was one of the fine 18th-century interiors destroyed in the fire

children to mingle like us, and to wander through the village and surrounding country.

My sister and I often look back to our involvement as children in reviving the house, perhaps most when in charge of buckets to catch the rain, or when laying a bottle with our names in it behind new work in the north wing. My family is no less supportive of the house now, because I think we have all learnt that houses are made of far more than just bricks and mortar.

A witness to history

'Truly this house of Long Melford, tho' it is not so great, yet it is so well compacted and contrived with such dainty conveniences every way, that if you saw the landskip of it, you would be mightily taken with it, and it would serve for a choice pattern to build and contrive a house by.'

James Howell, 1621

At first sight, Melford Hall looks like a typical Tudor country house. Tall chimneystacks and octagonal turrets dramatise its silhouette. The locally made bricks from which it was built have weathered to a mellow pink over the past 400 years. All seems untroubled in this quiet corner of Suffolk. But then you notice that the house has distinctly un-Tudor sash-windows. Unlike many English country houses, Melford has never hidden itself away from local life, but has always lain close to the heart of Long Melford, its huge village green. And it soon becomes apparent that quiet Melford Hall has in fact been touched by history – many times and sometimes savagely.

Melford Hall was built in the 16th century, but it is still not clear exactly when or by whom. Was it John Reeve, the high-spending last Abbot of the Benedictine monastery of St Edmundsbury, which had owned the manor of Melford since before the Norman Conquest? Or was it Sir William Cordell? He was one of the most able and ambitious 'new men' of the Elizabethan age, who acquired Melford after the Dissolution of the Monasteries and entertained the Queen here in 1578. The present building probably combines the work of both men.

In August 1642, as the Civil War was about to erupt, a mob descended on Melford Hall, smashing all the windows, looting the interior,

Melford Hall from the north-west in 1796; watercolour by Michael Angelo Rooker

The Blue Drawing Room fireplace

The outside of the house bears the scars of all these events lightly. Inside, it is a different story – both fascinating and complicated. Today, as you walk round the house, you move constantly from one style and period to another. The Hall retains the proportions of the Tudor original, but the ornate plasterwork ceiling it doubtless once had has long since gone. In the 1730s, the Firebraces modernised many of the principal rooms in the fashionable Rococo style. Much of their best work was lost in the 1942 fire, but you can still see curly Rococo fireplaces in the Blue Drawing Room and North Bedroom. In the early 19th century, the architect Thomas Hopper created a sophisticated Regency library and a grand new processional staircase. Later in that century, an antiquarian-minded Hyde Parker introduced much dark oak antique furniture. After the 1942 fire, the stylistic pendulum swung sharply back, when the present Baronet's Danish mother, Ulla, Lady Hyde Parker, introduced a refreshing breath of Scandinavian fresh air into the reconstructed rooms.

Melford remains a house to 'be mightily taken with'.

and leaving the cellars knee deep in beer. But Melford survived, to flourish again during the 18th century in the hands of the Cordells and their descendants, the Firebraces.

Since 1786 the house has been the home of the Hyde Parkers, one of Britain's most distinguished naval families. They have fought and died for their country in many of the great sea battles of Britain's maritime supremacy. Naval portraits and battle scenes and the spoils of those battles fill the house.

In 1942, exactly 300 years after the Civil War sacking of Melford, the house was devastated once more, when fire gutted the north wing. But again, despite the building restrictions of the austerity years, recovery was swift, and Melford was in good heart by the time it was transferred to the National Trust in 1960.

(Right) This Chinese famille rose dish came from the cargo of a Spanish vessel captured by Hyde Parker I in 1762

Tour of the House

The Approach

The house lies close to the centre of Long Melford, but turns its back on the village. To extend the approach drive, and increase its impressiveness, you enter the grounds from the village green at the north-west corner of the garden, and then proceed round two sides of the house before you finally reach the main entrance.

The pretty turreted entrance archway and flanking lodges were built by the 8th Baronet in 1838 in the same style as the house.

The Exterior

Melford is a tribute to the skill of the Tudor bricklayers. They required hundreds of thousands of bricks, which were made on site in temporary kilns or clamps. This gigantic enterprise is still remembered in the name of nearby Clampe Meadow.

The East (Entrance) Front

This front is dominated by the two tall octagonal turrets that face one another across the courtyard. They contain narrow spiral staircases which would have provided direct access not only to the first floor, but also to the roof of the vanished east range. (The blocked doorways can still be seen on the inner faces of the turrets at roof level.) This range (which is recorded on the 1613 Pierse map, illustrated on p. 28) originally connected the two wings, and would have provided the perfect viewing platform from which to observe the progress of the deer-hunt in the park beyond. It was demolished, along with a porter's lodge, in the early 18th century. Very similar turrets are also a feature of nearby Kentwell Hall, which was built about 1570.

(Right) The Renaissance-style Porch

None of the original windows seems to have survived, at least to the principal rooms. The wooden sash-windows were inserted in the early 18th century. More traditional stone mullions were restored to the ends of the wings and the Hall in the 19th century.

The Porch

A two-storey porch announces the principal entrance to the house. It bears the initials of Sir William Cordell and was always thought to have been built by him in the mid-16th century. There would have been a porch here in his time (recorded in the *c.*1606 Thorpe plan), but the initials look too fresh to be Elizabethan, and the break in the brickwork where the porch joins the main façade also suggests that it is a later addition. It was probably much damaged in the 1642 sack and rebuilt in a Tudor Renaissance style by the later Cordells, who may have recut

The Entrance Front

or added William Cordell's initials to gloss over the break in Cordell ownership. The Cordells probably also put up the rainwater heads, which are decorated with their cockatrice family crest. The rather awkwardly oversize sash-window in the porch was added in the 18th century.

The north wing (to the right) would originally have contained the principal family rooms and, on the first floor, the Great Chamber, where Cordell would have received the Queen and other honoured guests. The 1942 fire gutted this wing, entirely destroying the roof and bringing down the north-east corner of the outer wall. But thanks to the sensitivity of the restoration architect, Prof. Sir Albert Richardson, the devastation is hardly detectable today.

The south wing (to the left) originally contained the kitchen and other service rooms,

including the quarters for the steward of the estate. Since the 1970s, it has served as the family's private quarters.

The West (Garden) Front

Four more turrets tower above the roof line of the west elevation, and provide a suitably grand backdrop to the best garden, which was laid out in front of it.

(Right) The West Front

7

The Interior

The Hall

This was the Great Hall of the medieval house, where the whole household would have eaten, and important visitors would have been greeted and entertained.

In 1813 Thomas Hopper transformed the space into a Neo-classical 'stone' hall, adding such classical details as the huge early 18th-century-style fireplace, and the doorcases, ceiling cornice and wave moulding (or Vitruvian scroll) that runs round midway up the walls. He also took down the screen which would have separated the original entrance passage from the Hall, replacing it with two Doric columns to provide a suitably grand overture to his new staircase. Hopper's new central-heating system (see p. 18) helped to reduce the winter chill of this vast space.

In 1867 the 9th Baronet removed classical pediments from over the doors and installed the Jacobean panelling and the linenfold doors. His aim was to put back some of the room's earlier character and to create a suitable setting for his antique furniture and weapons.

The Hall remains a room for communal festivities.

Portraits

The *group of fine 17th-century portraits* has hung at Melford since the early 18th century, when they were fitted within fixed Rococo frames in the Dining Room. They came with the house

The Hall

when Sir Harry Parker bought it in 1786, and have always been thought to represent members of the Cordell family. However, the coats of arms are not those of the Cordells, and the identifying inscriptions were added only in the 18th century. Nor, in most cases, does the style of the picture match the dates of the suggested sitter. Despite this, these adopted 'ancestors' do help us to imagine what Melford's early owners would have looked like.

Also hanging here are portraits of the antiquarian 9th Baronet, *Sir William Parker*, shown appropriately in his library; his son, *the Rev. Sir William Hyde Parker, 10th Bt*, in clerical garb; and the present Baronet's father, *Sir William Hyde Parker, 11th Bt*, shown standing in front of Melford Hall, which he restored after the fire of 1942.

Wall-paintings

Set into the walls above the panelling is a series of *mythological scenes* painted in *grisaille* (shades of grey). They remain something of a mystery. Probably painted in the 17th

Beatrix Potter's watercolour sketch of the Hall fireplace

century, they were installed here either by the Firebraces in the early 18th century, or by Thomas Hopper as part of his remodelling of this room in the early 19th century.

Estate survey

Israel Amyce painted the large vellum map of the estate for Sir William Cordell in 1580. It includes a fairly crude representation from the south of the Tudor house, which emphasises its height, together with, to the right, the service buildings and outer gatehouses (now gone). In front of the house is the 'ponde yarde' with what may have been a pigeon house (also now gone) and three monastic fish-ponds, which still survive.

'Bulbous and uncomfortable'

'I think, on the whole, people in country houses had not much idea of period furniture. It was Jacobean and Elizabethan oak furniture, not at all beautiful, bulbous and uncomfortable. My husband's grandfather [the 9th Baronet] had collected an immense amount of antique furniture – heavy oak, the pieces one sees in the porch, and so on. A great deal was burnt in the fire – really a blessing in disguise!'

Ulla, Lady Hyde Parker

The Flemish firedogs are decorated with Biblical scenes, which are probably 17th-century, and the Cordell cockatrice crest (below)

Christmas tea in the Hall

'At Christmas-time we entertained every-body that we employed. We had over a hundred for Christmas tea, which started at three o'clock. It was a thing that I introduced, because in Denmark we make a lot of our Christmas…. Tea was laid out in the front hall. There was a big table for all the children, and an enormous Christmas tree, with a present for everybody. To begin with, everybody was very shy; then the party got going, and after they had had something to eat and the children had had their presents, they loosened up and got much gayer. And then the beer came, the barrels of beer, which were out in the back, and the butler would start pouring it out. He would then give everybody beer, the wives and the men, and they became quite gay. There was a grand piano in the hall, and somebody would play, and then they would start singing local Suffolk songs and speechifying.'

Ulla, Lady Hyde Parker

Sculpture

The naked *ivory figure* on the table is of the Christ Child and would originally have been clothed. It was carved in the 18th century by Chinese craftsmen in the Philippines for the Spanish market. Sir Hyde Parker I acquired it in 1762, when he captured the Spanish treasure galleon, the *Santissima Trinidad* (see p. 39).

Metalwork

In the fireplace is a pair of *Flemish firedogs*, decorated with panels depicting Biblical scenes,

(Right) A stained-glass panel of 1551 in the Hall depicting a praying nobleman and a bishop

The Hall in 1937

which are probably 17th-century. The bases, which bear the Cordell family crest of a cockatrice (a serpent-like monster) and the date 1559, seem to be antiquarianising 19th-century additions.

Furniture

The antiquarian 9th Baronet bought many of the old oak pieces here in the late 19th century as appropriate furnishings for an old house like Melford. One of the two *Nonsuch chests* is inscribed 1562. They are not a pair, but were made at the same time. The name is taken from Henry VIII's long-lost Nonsuch Palace in Surrey, which was once thought to be the building depicted in inlay on early examples. The *two oak court cupboards* are 19th-century interpretations of 17th-century pieces, turned out to satisfy collectors like the 9th Baronet.

The *longcase clock* was made by the Huguenot craftsman Thomas Grignion (d. 1784) of Covent Garden.

The *lozenge-shaped panel* hanging to the right of the far window bears the Cordell coat of arms, and was made to commemorate the death of Sir William Cordell's wife Mary in 1585. It is a very rare forerunner of the armorial hatchment, which was traditionally placed over the front door of country houses to announce the death of a member of the family. Many can still be seen hanging in churches.

Stained glass

The panels of stained glass inset into the windows are rare examples of 16th-century work, mostly English and Flemish. They were collected by the 9th Baronet, again to add antiquity to the decoration of his ancient home. They include the royal arms of Henry VII and his Queen, Elizabeth of York.

The Dining Room or Hyde Parker Room

This cool white room is in startling contrast to the Victorian Hall. The white-painted walls and uncarpeted, polished stone floor reflect the Scandinavian taste of Ulla, Lady Hyde Parker, who, with her husband, had to rebuild the room after it had been devastated by the 1942 fire. The fireplace is the one element that survived the fire, but sits well with the new decoration.

Before 1942, the room had looked very different. It had previously been an ante-room – part of the suite created in the 1730s by Sir Cordell Firebrace in the Rococo style, with luxuriantly curling scrolls on the fireplace, plasterwork ceiling, overdoors and fixed picture frames.

Every morning at ten in the 1930s, Ethel, Lady Hyde Parker would go across to the Kitchen and discuss the dining-room menus for the day with the cook. Much of the food came from the estate, including plenty of game and hams, which were cured with salt to a special recipe and then smoked over oak logs in an estate cottage.

Picture

Over the fireplace hangs *Catwyk on the Rhine*, a winter landscape painted in 1662, by Anthonie Beerstraeten (active 1639–71).

Portraits

Round the walls are displayed portraits of mostly 18th-century members of the Parker family. They include, clockwise from left of the fireplace, *John Parker, 1st Earl of Morley* (1772–1840), who lived at Saltram in Devon (now also the property of the National Trust); *Sir Henry Parker, 2nd Bt* (1639–1713); Captain (later Vice-Admiral) *Sir Hyde Parker, 5th Bt* (1713–83); and two portraits of *Sir Harry Parker, 6th Bt* (1735–1812), who bought Melford in 1786, together with his wife, *Bridget*.

(Right) Catwyk on the Rhine; by Anthonie Beerstraeten (Dining Room)

Furniture

The pair of *mid-18th-century pier-tables* was rescued from the fire, but lost their original marble tops and gilding. They were repainted white to suit the decoration of the new room. There is a matching pier-glass between the windows.

The five mahogany *tassel-backed chairs*, *c.*1730, are of particularly high quality. The five walnut *dining-chairs*, *c.*1740–60, are probably Irish and are among the pieces sketched by Beatrix Potter on a visit to Melford.

The *late Georgian dumb waiter* was so-called because it stood in for the servants after they had withdrawn from the room. The revolving trays held dessert and cutlery, to which diners could help themselves. In 1784 the diarist Mary Hamilton noted, 'We had dumb waiters so our conversation was not under any restraint by ye Servants being in ye room.'

The Blue Drawing Room

The Blue Drawing Room presents a much more traditional appearance than the Dining Room. Fortunately, the 1942 fire did not reach this room, which still has its early 18th-century decoration intact – Rococo carved-wood chimneypiece, simply panelled walls and block cornice. Before the fire, it was used as a dining room.

Pictures

From left of the entrance door are displayed: a pair of landscapes by J. C. Vollaert (1708–69); a pair of still-lives with birds by Jan van Kessel (1620–79); *The Finding of Moses* by Adriaen van Stalbemt (1580–1662); a flowerpiece by Pieter Gallis (1633–97); *The Christ Child and Angels* after Giovanni Battista Crespi (c.1575–1632); over the fireplace, *A Girl with a Lamb* (Margaret Parker, daughter of Sir Henry Parker, 2nd Bt); and five small portraits of members of the family of Hugh Parker (1672–1712), the 2nd Baronet's eldest son.

Furniture

The Louis XV *writing-table*, c.1770, is stamped with the name of Germain Landrin (d. 1785), a Paris cabinetmaker who specialised in smaller pieces veneered with exotic woods. The ceramic plaques with which it is decorated may have been added later.

The pair of *pole-screens* flanking the fireplace, c.1790, is decorated with fine needle-work. They were used to protect delicate complexions from the heat of the fire.

The *bureau on stand*, c.1740, was made in China of padoukwood, perhaps acquired by the Hyde Parkers in the late 18th century. The single *armchair* is late 19th-century.

The seaweed marquetry *longcase clock* was made c.1700 by Richard Street. It is a rare example of a 'year-going clock', which has to be wound only once a year.

A ceramic plaque from the Louis XV writing-table in the Blue Drawing Room

The Library

The Melford Library is a particularly handsome and complete example of Regency design, still preserving the bookcases and furniture that were made specially for it.

The room was created in 1813 by the architect Thomas Hopper for Sir William Parker, 7th Bt, by enclosing what had been an external portico on the west front. It is in fact two rooms, the smaller octagonal space being cleverly fitted between the inner turrets at the centre of the west front. The screen of columns disguises the division.

The decorative details are in the Greek Revival style, which was popular at the time. The anthemion frieze and the elegant Ionic columns were probably based on French 18th-century engravings of the Erectheum, one of the principal temples on the Acropolis in Athens. The columns look like solid marble, but are in fact hollow and made of scagliola, a compound of pulverised stone and plaster skilfully mixed and polished to resemble veined marble.

Portrait

Hanging over the fireplace in the small room is George Romney's fine portrait of *Vice-Admiral Sir Hyde Parker I, 5th Bt* (1713–83), whose son bought Melford. Sir Hyde came from a long line of gallant Parker naval officers. In the background is depicted the Battle of the Dogger Bank, in which on 5 August 1781 Sir Hyde's squadron confronted a Dutch fleet of equal strength. After a fierce exchange, both sides withdrew with honours even.

Furniture

The *bookcases in the larger room* are masterpieces of Regency cabinetwork, skilfully constructed from oak with yew wood and dark-stained walnut veneers to fit the curving walls of the room.

The *bookcases in the octagonal room* are rather different. They were made from rosewood with brass inlay and ormolu mounts, probably for the London house of the 1st Marquess of Hastings, for whom the 7th Baronet had worked as private secretary. He acquired them in 1826, after the rest of the Library was complete, as 'a memento of his former chief'. Making them fit this octagonal space produced some awkward joins.

The *movable furniture* was commissioned to complement the bookcases. Such grand Regency pieces went out of fashion in the late 19th century, when they were consigned to the attics, from where Ulla, Lady Hyde Parker rescued them in the 1930s.

The *suite of three library tables and an upright screen* in pale oak, yew and ebonised walnut, was made *c.*1814, probably by the fashionable New Bond Street firm of Morant & Co. The tables are supported on large paw feet, which were inspired by a classical sarcophagus and which also appear in the Library grates. The four oak *library chairs* have owls carved on the arms – an appropriate motif for a classically inspired library, as the owl was the symbol of Minerva, the Greek goddess of wisdom. The fifth *armchair* is rosewood with brass inlay (like the four single chairs) and probably arrived at the same time as the rosewood bookcases. The pair of *'Grecian couches'* is supported by eagles – another bird favoured by classical designers – and has been attributed to Gillows of Lancaster, equally successful furniture-makers of the period.

The *ebony and ivory box* on the table was made *c.*1750 in Vizagapatam on the east coast of India, which specialised in turning out this kind of ornately inlaid work for the export trade.

(Right) The Greek Revival frieze in the Library

Restoring the Library
Hopper was a better architect than he was an engineer, as his modernisation of the interior of Melford caused serious structural problems. When the Library was dismantled for repair in 1979, it was discovered that the entire weight of one of the inner turret walls was resting precariously on Hopper's hollow columns. At the same time, the floor structure was repaired, and the walls repainted in their original colours of pink and raw sienna.

Books

The books are typical of a gentleman's library of the 18th and early 19th centuries. Many bear the bookplate of the 7th Baronet, who created this room. There is a good group of books on natural history and gardening, including Redouté and de Candolle's *Plantarum Succulentarum Historia* (1799), with particularly fine hand-coloured plates. As you would expect in such a distinguished naval family, naval history and theory are well represented, with a long, late 18th-century run of the *Nautical Almanac*.

Ceramics

Above the bookcases is some of the **Chinese famile rose export porcelain** of the Qianlong period, *c.*1755–60, taken as a prize by Captain Hyde Parker I, when he captured the *Santissima Trinidad*.

15

Battle paintings by Dominic Serres in the Library

The American War of Independence

13 July 1776: *The Passage of the Hudson River*
Captain Hyde Parker II, in command of the frigate *Phoenix* with the *Rose* and the *Tryal*, exchanging fire with batteries at Manhattan and the opposite bank after penetrating the Hudson River. The ships are flying the flags of Admiral Shuldham, whose squadron was stationed off New York to confront the rebel colonists. Shuldham was succeeded by Admiral Howe, whose flag is shown in some of the other Serres paintings. Painted in 1777.

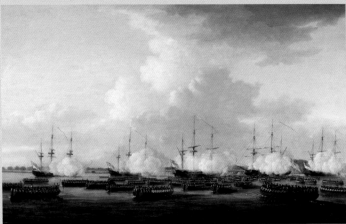

4 August 1776: *Action off Tarrytown*
Hyde Parker II's flotilla (now under the flag of Admiral Howe) sailed further up the Hudson towards Tarrytown, where they were attacked by rebels in longboats. Painted in 1779.

16 August 1776: *American Fireships on the Hudson*
The enemy attacked at night with fireships, one of which became entangled with the *Phoenix* (on the left). After 45 minutes Hyde Parker II managed to douse the flames sufficiently to extricate himself and return down river to New York with his force. Painted in 1777.

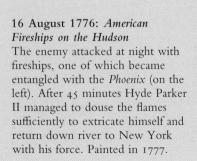

9 October 1776: *Forcing the Boom on the Hudson River*

In September 1776 British forces captured the southern end of Manhattan from the rebels. The following month Hyde Parker II led a second flotilla up the Hudson, across which the rebels had meanwhile thrown a defensive boom. The *Phoenix*, with the frigates *Tartar* and *Roebuck*, is shown breaking through the boom and returning fire from Forts Washington and Lee. In 1778 Hyde Parker II returned to Britain, where he was knighted for his exploits. Painted in 1779.

Fighting the French

25 March 1780: *A British Squadron off St Lucia*

Rear-Admiral Sir Hyde Parker I commanded a squadron in the Caribbean defending the island of St Lucia against the French. Although the French commander, the comte de Guichen, had a numerically superior force, he withdrew when he found that Parker's fleet had instantly slipped anchor and formed line of battle to meet him – the remarkable feat of seamanship recorded in this picture. Painted in 1781.

4 October 1780: *The Shipwreck of the Phoenix at Night*

Sir Hyde Parker II returned to the West Indies in the *Phoenix* in 1780, but was caught at sea in a hurricane. The *Phoenix* was driven ashore on the hostile coast of Cuba and wrecked. Despite the storm and the darkness, Hyde Parker managed to rescue most of his crew and much of the *Phoenix*'s stores and armaments. Painted in 1781.

Fighting the Dutch

5 August 1781: *The Battle of the Dogger Bank*

In March 1781 Admiral Hyde Parker I was appointed to command a North Sea squadron of six elderly battleships. While escorting a convoy of 200 merchant vessels that August, he encountered a similar Dutch force under Rear-Admiral Johan Arnold Zoutman. A fierce, but inconclusive battle followed. Although Parker had acquitted himself well, he was so unhappy with the state of his squadron that he resigned, arguing that the Royal Navy needed better ships and younger commanders (he was 67 at the time). Painted in 1782.

The Stairs

Hopper designed the Stairs to provide a grand processional route from his remodelled Hall to the first floor. In order to create the space needed to accommodate this single, straight cascade of steps, broken only by a broad half-landing, he had to sweep away whatever survived of the dog-leg staircase shown on John Thorpe's early 17th-century plan (see p. 34). At the top of stairs, he inserted two screens of Ionic columns, which support a shallow barrel ceiling decorated with recessed coffering.

Hopper's new staircase was in the austere French Neo-classical style. He seems to have borrowed the idea from the main stairs in the palais de Luxembourg in Paris (now the French Senate), which were designed in 1795 by Jean-François Chalgrin, architect of the Arc de Triomphe.

Portraits

At the bottom of the stairs, are, to the right, *Sir Cordell Firebrace, 3rd Bt* (1712–59), who remodelled several of the principal rooms in the Rococo style in the 1730s; and, to the left, a late 17th-century portrait, inscribed as of *Sir John Cordell, 3rd Bt* (1677–1704).

Hanging over the stairs is Romney's impressive full-length portrait of *Captain Sir Hyde Parker II, Kt* (1739–1807), who was to be Nelson's commanding officer at the Battle of Copenhagen in 1801 (see p. 39).

Ceramics

The three *cabinets* at the bottom of the stairs display, to the left, Chinese export dinner plates in order of date from *c*.1720–*c*.1755. To the right are part services made in China for the Parker and Leslie families. In the far right case are Chinese ceramics from the *Santissima Trinidad*.

The Boudoir

This room still has most of the panelling installed by Sir Cordell Firebrace in the 1730s. In the 1830s the room served as a billiard room. It now makes a surprisingly modest focus for Hopper's grand new stairs. At some point, the ceiling was raised – hence the strangely extended cornice. The Boudoir could be shut off from the Gallery with double-doors, later removed.

Furniture

The *two Italian side-chairs* on the left were made about 1860 in a mid-18th-century style and are the remains of a set that was largely destroyed in the fire. They are decorated with the crest of the House of Savoy in northern Italy, which provided the kings of Italy from 1861 to 1946. The mahogany *square piano*, *c*.1800, is a Broadwood. There is also a fine 18th-century satinwood *games table*.

Ceramics

In the cabinets on the left-hand wall are a pair of large *Meissen vases*, *c*.1860, and parts of two *dinner services* – on the left, Fürstemberg, *c*.1770, and, on the right, large Meissen soup tureens and stands in the Neubrandenstein pattern, *c*.1755.

Heating the house

Melford was one of the earliest country houses in Britain to have central heating. The *circular brass grilles* on the landings were supplied in 1813 by Moser & Co. of Soho as part of Hopper's modernisation of the house. The new system was designed to supplement, rather than replace, the existing open fires, and was restricted to the main rooms. According to the historian Christina Hardyment, 'central heating in bedrooms was regarded as positively depraved'.

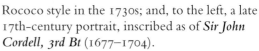

The Stairs in 2005

Going to Market; by Jan Siberechts (Gallery)

The Gallery

Hopper had to work within the Elizabethan fabric and with the limited number of existing windows, but he still managed to devise a grand and subtle setting for his staircase. The cast-iron balustrade which runs behind the columns has a Louis XVI-style pattern of linked chains.
The floor is plain oak parquet – again French in inspiration.

Pictures

Along the right-hand side of the Gallery hangs an encampment scene attributed to Benjamin Gerritz. Cuyp (1612–52), flanked by *A Water Mill* attributed to Van der Jull and *Horses, Sheep and Cattle before a Cottage* in the manner of Paulus Potter (1625–54).

On the left side of the Gallery are *Going to Market*, painted in 1662 by Jan Siberechts

(1627–1703), *Sportsmen at an Inn* after Adriaen van Ostade (1610–85), and *Landscape with a Riding School* after Philips Wouwerman (1619–68).

The female portrait is of the tragic *Elizabeth, Countess Rivers* (1581–1651). A loyal Catholic supporter of Charles I, she died in debtors' prison, having seen Melford ransacked by a Puritan mob.

Furniture

The bench under the stained-glass window is made from the timbers of a whale-boat from HMS *Firebrand*, which was commanded by Captain Hyde Parker, who was killed in 1854 during the Crimean War.

The Chapel

The Chapel remains in use. This narrow room lies above the Porch and in the early 17th century would have formed part of Lady Savage's sitting room. Hopper carved up this space to make his new staircase. The Rev. Sir

Stained glass

Queen Elizabeth I visited Melford in 1578 (see p. 33). She is depicted here in the blue dress she wore to the service which was held in old St Paul's Cathedral in November 1588 to give thanks for the defeat of the Spanish Armada. Verses said to have been written by her at the time acknowledged God's help in the victory:

> *He made the wynds and waters rise*
> *To scatter all myne enemyes.*

William Hyde Parker converted the room into a chapel. Ulla, Lady Hyde Parker was a member of an Anglican order of nuns in Oxford.

Ivory

The ivory figure of the *Virgin Mary* was made in the Spanish Philippines in the mid-18th century, and like the Christ Child in the Hall, came from the cargo of the *Santissima Trinidad*.

The Nursery

This room used to be Nanny Kitchen's bed-room. It is now a nursery filled with family toys from William Hyde Parker's Lego to Jemima Puddle-Duck, gifted to the Hyde Parker children by their cousin Beatrix Potter.

(Far right) This toy Jemima Puddle-Duck was given to the Hyde Parker children by Beatrix Potter

(Right) A mid-18th- century Philippino ivory of Our Lady of the Immaculate Conception. She stands on a crescent moon with her foot on a serpent's head, symbolising her triumph over evil. She originally had a gold and diamond-studded halo, gold and ruby earrings, and a gold and emerald ring. These were stolen in 1915

Paintings

The Hungarian artist Felix Harta painted the watercolours of Sir Richard and his sister Elisabeth along with the pastel of their nanny, Sybil Kitchen. Colourful collages depict scenes from Hans Christian Anderson's fairy tales: *The Princess and the Pea*, *The Shepherdess and the Chimney Sweep*, *The Brave Tin Soldier* and *The Emperor's New Suit*. They were made by Ivor Ditlef-Nielsen, younger brother of Ulla, Lady Hyde Parker.

Furniture

The *painted shield-back chairs*, c.1790, are in the style of George Seddon.

'Cousin Beattie' at Melford

'When at Melford, Cousin Beattie had not spoken a great deal to the children, though she read her stories to them to find out their reactions. Most of her time had been spent out of doors drawing and painting. She drew some of the Jeremy Fisher illustrations at our ancient fish-ponds, and while there she sketched Melford as seen over these ponds. (This book is dedicated to Stephanie Hyde Parker.)'

Ulla, Lady Hyde Parker

The West Corridor

A fragment of a late 19th-century stencilled frieze has been revealed opposite the West Bedroom. Its murky green colours and black pattern are representative of the dark decoration that Ulla, Lady Hyde Parker, would have encountered when she first came to Melford Hall. The colours on the doors are a recreation of a striking 19th-century scheme.

Pictures

Along the West Corridor are a series of illustrations and watercolours of Melford Hall, painted by Beatrix Potter.

Furniture

The *mirror* in the showcase dates to the 17th-century. Its surround is embellished with raised embroidery known as *stumpwork*. The figures represent four of the five senses (hearing, touch, smell and taste) and the mirror itself represents the fifth sense, sight.

Ceramics

The *showcase* contains a selection of mostly Kangxi *famille verte* dishes, c.1720, and Qianlong *famille rose*, c.1750.

The West Bedroom

Beatrix Potter stayed in this room when she visited Melford. She kept her travelling menagerie of animals in the smaller turret room.

The colours and furnishings are based on 19th-century evidence: an inventory taken in 1846 lists chintz window curtains 'with painted cornice'. The silk bed hangings were inspired by a Beatrix Potter sketch of a white mouse sleeping in this room.

(Right) A chair back, c.1860, in the West Bedroom made from papier mâché embellished with mother-of-pearl

Many of the contents were chosen for the room by Ulla, Lady Hyde Parker.

Furniture

The set of *three tables* (originally four) and the *chair*, c.1860, are made of papier mâché decorated with engravings and mother-of-pearl. The technique, which was introduced to Britain by the 1670s, involves mixing pulped paper with glue, moulding to shape, hardening and polishing. It became particularly popular in the Victorian period, when Birmingham manufacturers produced papier-mâché tea-trays by the thousand. But it also proved strong enough for use in light tables and chairs of this kind. The *embroidered rug* at the foot of the bed was worked by Ulla, Lady Hyde Parker.

The West Bedroom

The *portrait* over the mantelpiece depicts Eliza Leech, aunt of Beatrix Potter and mother of Ethel Leech, who married Sir William Hyde Parker in 1890. The *bed* belonged to Ulla, Lady Hyde Parker, and was formerly in the North Wing.

The North Dressing Room

This was Sir Richard's dressing room in the 1970s. The prints are of Admiral Lord Horatio Nelson and his mistress Lady Emma Hamilton.

(Left)
The North
Bedroom

(Right)
Venus and
Cupid;
a painted-
glass panel on
the early
17th-century
Italian cabinet

The North Bedroom

In the mid-19th century this room was known as the Green Room. The name is supported by the recent discovery of a layer of rich green paint, which has been matched and reused on the walls. The bed hangings, curtains and carpet were placed in the room by Ulla, Lady Hyde Parker. Before the Second World War the carpet was in the Dining Room and is one of the few to have survived the fire.

Pictures

The two large portraits are of *Sir Charles Firebrace, Bt* (1680–1727) and his wife *Margaret* (née Cordell), who owned Melford Hall in the early 1700s.

Furniture

The mirror *overmantel* in this room incorporates Rococo carving salvaged after the 1942 fire from elsewhere in the house. The early 17th-century Italian *cabinet* on stand is decorated with panels of *verre églomisé* (painted glass) depicting gods and goddesses – probably the work of

The Rococo overmantel in the North Bedroom combines fragments rescued from elsewhere in the house

contained a grand drawing room, saloon, a Pre-Reformation stair and suites of bedrooms and dressing rooms.

The Red Bedroom

The fire in the North Wing spread from the fireplace in this room when hot ashes were raked out onto the hearth. The fireplace has a stone surround designed by Prof. Sir Albert Richardson in a style common to all fireplaces in the restored wing. The room was decorated by Ulla, Lady Hyde Parker, and was used as a guest bedroom.

Portraits

Above the fireplace hangs a portrait of *Ulla, Lady Hyde Parker*, by Felix Albrecht Harta.

Furniture

Two painted French-style *armchairs* (on loan from Stourhead).

Neapolitan craftsmen. The *bed* came from Blickling Hall in Norfolk, for which it was bought by Lord Lothian. Three more of the painted *shield-back chairs* are shown here. The red lacquer *mirror* is on loan from the Fitzwilliam Museum in Cambridge.

The North Wing

The entire wing was gutted by fire in 1942 during military occupation. It was subsequently restored as a self-contained family home by Prof. Sir Albert Richardson. The windows were retained in their original positions but the internal walls were repositioned to suit a smaller room arrangement. Prior to the fire, the wing

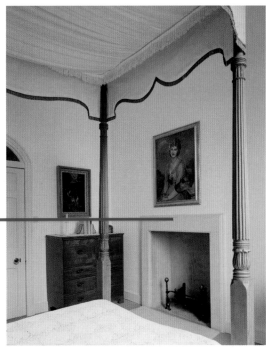

The Red Bedroom

The Upper North Corridor

Before the fire the principal bedroom on the first floor of the North Wing contained an intricately carved Tudor bedstead. Prof. Sir Albert Richardson's corridor terminates at the north end with an oval lobby giving access to two rooms used as Bedrooms by Ulla, Lady Hyde Parker.

Paintings

Along the Upper North Corridor there are several pen and ink drawings by Beatrix Potter. In the oval lobby, a series of Russian icons bought by Ulla, Lady Hyde Parker, are displayed.

The North Stairs

The stairwell was designed as the axis of the restored wing. The staircase came from another country house and was installed by Prof. Sir Albert Richardson. Before the fire, this space and the current tea room were part of a drawing room designed by Thomas Hopper c.1840.

Paintings

Here hangs a portrait in oil of *Sir Henry Parker, 2nd Bt* (1638–1713) of Honington Hall, Warwickshire, whose great-grandson, Sir Harry Parker, 6th Bt, purchased the Melford estate in 1786.

The Lower North Corridor

Here the Scandinavian influence of Ulla, Lady Hyde Parker is most noticeable and the group of unframed oil paintings creates a dramatic contrast with the white walls. The corridor is flooded with light from the south-facing windows, which would once have been part of the Drawing Room.

The suit of armour is a 19th-century replica of a 16th-century German suit of armour (on loan from the Victoria and Albert Museum).

Paintings

The painting of Classical ruins (school of Panini) was in a Rococo plaster frame over the fireplace in the Dining Room until it was saved from the fire. The large unframed oil painting of a peasant banquet in a barn is in the manner of Jan Steen (1626–79).

The two 17th-century embroidered panels depict scenes from the Bible. On the right is a stumpwork panel showing Susanna and the Elders (from the Apocrypha) and to the left is a needlework of angels appearing to Abraham and Sarah (from the book of Genesis).

The Park Room
(*overflow tea room*)

Evidence revealed by the fire and a recently discovered inventory of 1635 points to this area forming the east end of a pre-reformation chapel. Before the fire this end of the North Wing formed a double-height saloon with a large bow window to the north overlooking the garden and park. The saloon was designed by Thomas Hopper c.1840. More recently this room was used as a drawing room by Ulla, Lady Hyde Parker.

Paintings

Oil painting of a village scene with feasting and merrymaking, by J.C. Droochsloot, 1653.

(Left) Close view of the carvings and turned wood railings of the North Wing staircase

(Right) The North Corridor

The Garden and Park

The garden occupies a flat site squeezed between the village to the west and the deer-park to the east. Despite the constricted setting, it has developed over the centuries into a place of beauty and variety.

The garden in 1613

The first reliable visual record we have of the garden and park is Samuel Pierse's estate map of 1613, which was prepared for Thomas Savage, perhaps as part of his revival of the estate. It shows a highly symmetrical arrangement typical of the period. The garden around the house was essentially square, defined by an outer wall and moat, which was fed by the nearby River Chad. At this date, the moat must have been more for show than protection. It certainly failed to stop the looters who attacked the house in 1642.

Within the outer wall, the garden was divided into further rectangular, walled compartments. To the south were the stables and other service buildings with their own courtyards, where laundry would have been hung to dry. They overlooked three large fish-ponds, which doubtless dated back to monastic times. Between the ponds Pierse

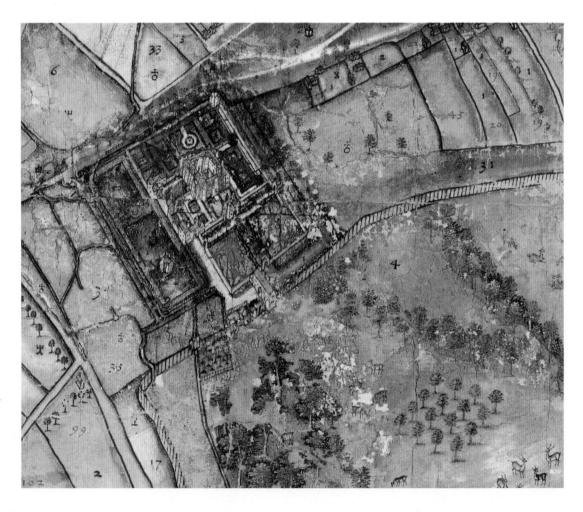

> 'For the gardening and choice of flowers, for fruits of all sorts, there are few the like in England. Here you have your Bon Christian pears and Bergamot in perfection; your Muscatel grapes in such plenty that there are some bottles of wine sent every year to the king.'
>
> James Howell, 1621

shows a little pavilion (now gone), which may have been the pigeon house recorded in William Cordell's will.

To the east were two walled forecourts, each with its own gatehouse, through which you would have passed to reach the main entrance to the house. The porter's lodge and its wall disappeared in the early 18th century, but John Thorpe's survey of *c.*1606 includes a pencil sketch of it.

On the north side of the house was a formal garden, which matched in size the stable courtyards on the opposite side of the house. From their rooms in the north wing, the family would have enjoyed good views over this garden, which comprised two square parterres and a bowling green with trees at the corners.

To the west was another larger formal garden, with more square parterres flanking a circular pond, which served as the overflow for the water supply. At the centre of the pond there may have been a statue or fountain.

The banqueting house

At the north-west corner of the west garden Pierse shows a little banqueting pavilion, which still stands as the principal survival of the early garden. Octagonal in plan, it was built of the same red brick as the house with pretty little gables. The banqueting house was once thought to have played a central part in the entertainments surrounding the 1578 royal visit to

(Left) Samuel Pierse's 1613 bird's-eye view shows the formal garden which the Savages created around the house

(Right) The banqueting house

Melford, but it is too far from the house to have been convenient for this, and it is not shown on the 1580 Amyce survey. It was probably built by the Savages in the early 17th century at the same time as they were making major changes to the west front of the house.

It was still grandly furnished for entertaining in 1635, when it contained a marble table and five giltwood chairs. The panelling and sash-windows were installed in the 18th century, together with the furnace on the ground floor, which fed a network of heating pipes, perhaps so that the pavilion could be used as an orangery.

The park

The park dates well back into medieval times and was much favoured by the more worldly abbots of St Edmundsbury, who loved to watch deer-hunts here. The abbots' 'Little Park' was enclosed in 1613 as part of the Savages' 'New Park'.

In Pierse's map, the deer-park is shown as separated from the garden to the west by a high paling fence. It was well wooded, with hides on stilts among the trees, from which one could shoot game. At the bottom right of the detail illustrated on p. 28, you can see an avenue of trees running diagonally north-east from opposite the entrance front to meet another, longer avenue that runs east-west. A version of these features was replanted in 1985.

Melford Hall and its owners

Monastic Melford

From before 1065 until 1539, the manor of Melford belonged to the great Benedictine abbey of St Edmundsbury (today known as Bury St Edmunds), which was one of the richest monasteries in Britain. In 1086 the Domesday Book recorded that the Melford estate comprised 1,500–2,000 acres. Throughout the Middle Ages, Melford was a prosperous place, a country estate reserved for the private enjoyment of the abbot. It was famous for its well-stocked deer-park and its pack of hounds. Abbot Sampson (1182–1211) did not hunt himself, but 'lyked moche to sytte in a stylle place in ye Melford woodes to see ye Abbey dogges honte ye stagges'.

By 1442, when Lord William Curteys was abbot, there was already a substantial house at Melford, described as a 'manor house with moats, ditches, gardens and pastures'. The early history of the present building is still unclear, but it is now thought that much of the external fabric may date from the 1510s. Soon after John

The boy king Henry VI prays at the shrine of St Edmund in 1433. The shrine made the abbey of St Edmundsbury one of the richest in Britain, and its abbot, William Curteys, became a trusted adviser to the King

Reeve was elected abbot in 1514, he seems to have embarked on a major campaign of rebuilding. He had a reputation for extravagance, if we are to believe the King's Commissioner for the Suppression of Religious Houses (not an unbiased source, admittedly): 'It was detected that he laye moche forth in his granges: that he delited moche in playing at dice and cardes, and therein spent moche money, and in building for his pleasure.' Reeve was a proud native of Long Melford and keen to outdo the most powerful local family, the Cloptons of Kentwell Hall. Early Tudor architectural patrons like Reeve realised that the way to impress was to build high. Melford's six tall turrets rise to little domes, which feature semicircular shell-patterned gables, an Italian Renaissance motif also found on the gatehouse of Layer Marney in Essex, which was built in the early 1520s. Massive red-brick gatehouses were the status symbol of the age, from the Base Court of Cardinal Wolsey's Hampton Court to St John's College, Cambridge. The central bay of Melford's now lost east front would have had just such a gatehouse, and before that range was demolished, the house would have had a similarly collegiate feel, with sets of self-contained rooms opening on to an enclosed central courtyard.

Like Wolsey, Abbot Reeve did not have long to enjoy his new mansion before it was confiscated by Henry VIII. When the monasteries were dissolved in the 1530s, the abbey of St Edmundsbury was too rich a prize to ignore. In 1535 Reeve had let Melford Hall and 148 acres to Dame Frances Pennington, in an attempt to preserve the estate from confiscation, although he was careful to retain the use of 'on[e] of the Best Chambers within the seyd manour'. But it did no good. On 4 November 1539, he, his prior and the remaining 42 monks signed the final document surrendering Melford Hall to the Crown.

The Cordells and Firebraces of Melford

John Cordell = Emma Webbe   = ?

Sir WILLIAM CORDELL, MP = Mary Clopton   JANE = Richard Allington
(?1522–81)   (d. 1585)   (d. 1602) | (d. 1561)
granted Melford Hall 1554

Sir Thomas Cordell

Mary = Sir John Savage, Bt
(d. 1635) | (d. 1615) m. before 1577

Sir THOMAS, VISCOUNT SAVAGE = Elizabeth Darcy   Sir John Cordell =
(c.1586–1635) | (1581–1651) m. 1602   (d. 1649)
cr. Viscount 1626 | cr. Countess Rivers 1641

Sir JOHN, = (1) Catherine Parker, dau. of Lord Monteagle, granddau. of Sir Thomas Tresham
EARL RIVERS,   (2) Mary Ogle
MP
(1603–54)
sells Melford to ROBERT CORDELL = Margaret Wright
1649 (c.1616–80) | (d. 1680) m. c.1643
cr. Bt 1660

Sir JOHN CORDELL, 2nd Bt = Elizabeth Waldegrave
(1646–90) | (d. 1709)

Sir JOHN CORDELL, 3rd Bt   MARGARET = Sir CHARLES FIREBRACE, 2nd Bt
(1677–1704)   (1675–1712) | (1680–1727)
m. 1710

(1) Sir CORDELL FIREBRACE, 3rd Bt = Bridget Evers = (3) Lord William Campbell
(1712–59) m. 1737   (d. 1782)   (d. 1787) m. 1762
           sells Melford to Sir Harry Parker, 6th Bt 1786

Owners of Melford Hall in CAPITALS

Sir William Cordell (?1522–81)

A new man

Cordell was one of the Tudor 'new men' who transformed 16th-century society. Like Abbot Reeve, he was a local Long Melford boy. His father has been a servant to Sir William Clopton of nearby Kentwell Hall, and the young William was brought up in the Clopton household. His abilities were recognised early, as at the age of about sixteen he was sent to Lincoln's Inn to study law – the route to riches for bright young men like him. He rapidly became a successful lawyer, being appointed Solicitor-General in 1553 and Master of the Rolls in 1557, when he was not yet 40. He also served as an MP under four monarchs. As a Catholic, he naturally found favour with Queen Mary, who knighted him and chose him to be Speaker in her final parliament in 1558 – the last Catholic to hold this office until the present incumbent, Michael Martin. Despite his faith and his service to Mary, he remained a respected figure under the Protestant Queen Elizabeth.

In time-honoured fashion, Cordell translated the profits of the law into land, buying up property across Suffolk. He also secured his new social position as a landed gentleman by an advantageous marriage to Sir William Clopton's granddaughter Mary, who was heiress to estates in Yorkshire and Lincolnshire. He started leasing Melford in the late 1540s, and was finally granted the property outright by Queen Mary in November 1554. Cordell was once thought to have built most of the present house, but he may have been content to make mostly fairly minor changes to Abbot Reeve's creation. His initials appear on the two-storey entrance porch at the centre of the east front, which was designed in a sophisticated French Renaissance style complete with Doric and Ionic pilasters. However, this is probably – at best – merely a mid-17th-century re-creation of whatever existed in Cordell's time, as the house was badly damaged in the 1642 pillage.

The 1580 map of Melford appears to show a rectangular house of four ranges laid out around a central courtyard. Cordell's will written the same year refers to his 'mansion house, commonly called or known by the name of Melford Hall' and also to 'that house commonly called the Old House, adjoining to the said capital messuage', which was probably the medieval home farm. This may be the building shown to the right of the main house on the 1580 map and to the east of the south service range on the 1613 Pierse survey.

Cordell died a wealthy man in 1581. In his will he proudly recorded that the revenue from Melford 'is much more than ever any of my ancestors (to my understanding) ever had'. He had already returned some of his wealth to his native village, in 1573 endowing the row

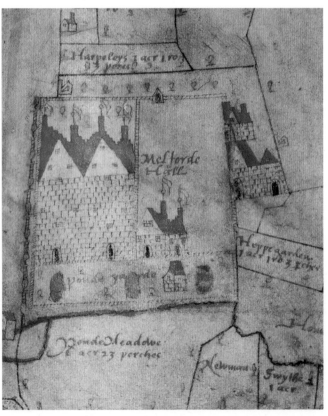

(Right) Sir William Cordell's Melford Hall as shown on Israel Amyce's estate map of 1580

Cordell instructed that a monument should be erected to him in Long Melford church within two years of his death. He had fallen out with his wife Mary, who is not represented on it

of almshouses that still stands on the green. In his will, Cordell also left money for a monument to himself in Long Melford church. The magnificent result was the work of Cornelius Cure, a leading London sculptor of the time, who was chosen by Cordell's sister and executor, Jane Allington. Standing over his effigy are the figures symbolising the cardinal virtues of Temperance, Prudence, Justice and Fortitude. Fortitude was a sadly appropriate choice, as all four of Cordell's children had died young. For all his worldly success, he had failed to found a new dynasty at Melford, although Cordell cousins were to buy back the house in 1649.

After Mary Cordell's death in 1585, Melford passed to Jane Allington, who seems to have lived mostly in London and to have neglected the house. Shortly before her death in 1602, *The Chorography of Suffolk* had noted that Melford Hall 'beginneth to be ruinous'.

A royal visit

Cordell was one of the most hospitable country gentlemen in Suffolk. So when the Queen made a summer progress into the county in 1578, it was natural that she should stay at Melford. The Queen's Gentleman Usher Symon Bowyer, who preceded the royal party, spent two days decorating two temporary banqueting houses in the garden with gold and silver brought up specially from her Jewel House in London. Even so, there were some anxious moments after the Queen arrived on the evening of 2 August, as she was not happy with the decorations. Her servants had to race back to London to bring 'certayne riche Cuppes, standing Trenchers and Salte of golde and other thinges'. For Melford was the setting for a critical meeting with the French ambassador, de Bacqueville, who was acting as an envoy for the duc d'Alençon. D'Alençon was one of the Queen's most ardent suitors, and although she had no intention of marrying him, she was anxious to impress his representative. In the event, the meeting seems to have gone smoothly. When the Queen left, Cordell presented her with 'a cup of golde, the cover and foote enamuled with eight course diamonds and in the top of the cover a fair emeraude and another cup of golde enameled like tother emerald'.

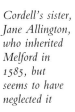

Cordell's sister, Jane Allington, who inherited Melford in 1585, but seems to have neglected it

Sir Thomas Savage (c.1586–1635)

On her death, Jane Allington bequeathed Melford to her grandson, Thomas Savage, who came from an ancient Cheshire family. In the same year Savage married Elizabeth Darcy, a fellow Catholic and an heiress. It was a love match, and a productive one: over the next 28 years they were to have nineteen children. 'I never saw such a dainty race of children in all my life', wrote their tutor, James Howell.

Like Cordell, Thomas Savage was trained from an early age as a lawyer. In 1597, when still only about eleven, he was described as:

> Pleasant in show, discreet beyond his years
> Well spoken, courteous and judicial.

Savage quickly established himself at the court of James I, becoming a friend of the King's most powerful courtier, the Duke of Buckingham. Henry, Prince of Wales was godfather to the Savages' eldest child, who was born in 1603. Savage in return kept the King well supplied with wine made from muscatel grapes grown at Melford. But, as a Catholic, he was disbarred from holding any senior office. His position improved under Charles I, who appointed him Chancellor of the Household to Queen Henrietta Maria, who was herself a Catholic. Elizabeth Savage also served as a lady-in-waiting to the Queen, and covertly celebrated Mass with her. Savage was created a viscount in 1626.

By the early 17th century, Abbot Reeve's house was almost a century old, and the Savages began contemplating improvements. A plan drawn up about 1606 by the surveyor John Thorpe seems to show their intentions. The house had always been short of bedrooms, and to accommodate their rapidly growing family, the Savages may have added the three-storey blocks at the corners of the west front. They were to need both 'Great and Little Nurseries'. Melford had hitherto also lacked that mark of the great Elizabethan house, a long gallery. Savage inserted one above the Great Hall, and hung 23 pictures 'of sundry sizes' in it.

Thomas Savage's grandmother seems to have removed most of Cordell's furniture, and so he set about completely refurnishing the house in the style of the time. The 1635 inventory reveals that the main rooms were hung with tapestries. The Great Chamber and the adjacent Withdrawing Chamber contained nine scenes from the Old Testament story of Absalom. The total effect must have been both rich and colourful: Thomas Savage's bedroom was decked out in green, and there were also Purple and Gold Bedchambers. The inventory also notes that the cellars contained no fewer than 2,887 gallons of beer.

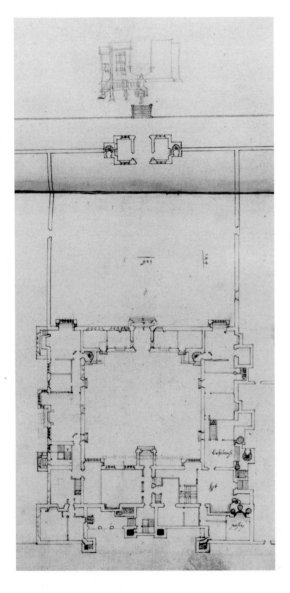

(Left) John Thorpe's survey of Melford Hall about 1606

Viscount Savage died at his London house in 1635 of 'the running gout'. His body was taken north to be buried in the Savage family chapel in Macclesfield. The funeral was lavish, but there was to be no grand monument, as the Savages' refurnishing of Melford had racked up debts of £14,000.

Elizabeth Savage, Countess Rivers (1581–1651)

Viscount Savage's widow Elizabeth was left almost penniless on his death. She badgered the King to help her, but with little success. Her cousin John Cordell described her unkindly as 'an impecunious but ingenious courtier on the make'. Despite this, she remained a lady of the bedchamber to Henrietta Maria until at least 1641, when she was created Countess Rivers in her own right. However, grand titles do not pay the bills, her son John was also deep in debt, and life was getting increasingly difficult for Catholics. In November 1641 she was obliged to mortgage the Melford estate for £15,000 to John Cordell and his son Robert, who were prosperous London mercers descended from Sir William Cordell's grandfather.

Lady Rivers retreated to her old family home at St Osyth Priory in Essex, but the respite was to be brief. In August 1642, as the King's authority was being increasingly challenged, a mob began attacking the homes of his largely Catholic supporters in Essex and Suffolk. Lady Rivers was an obvious target. On 22 August

Elizabeth, Countess Rivers

rioters ransacked St Osyth Priory, forcing her to flee to Melford, where she still had the use of the house. Two days later, the mob caught up with her. The diarist John Rous described what happened next:

The lady Savage's house was defaced; all glass broken, all iron pulled out, all household stuff gone, all ceilings rent down or spoiled, all likely places where money might be hidden dug up, the gardens defaced, beer and wine consumed, and let out (to knee deep in the cellar), the deer killed and chased out, etc. The lady saith the loss is £40,000.

Lady Rivers survived, but her last years were wretched. In early 1650 she was arrested for debt in London and sent to prison, where she died on 6 March 1651. In an epitaph, a friend described her as 'a beauty fell in winter's power'.

Her son, Sir John, 2nd Earl Rivers, was also arrested for debt, and had no choice but to sell Melford in 1649 to Robert Cordell. (The 2nd Earl's trustees confirmed the purchase, for £28,959, after his death in 1654.) In 1649 a visitor to Long Melford 'saw a sad divided town; I saw the ruines of that great [house] plundered out desolate without inhabitant'.

The frontispiece of the royalist tract Mercurius Rusticus illustrates the plundering of Melford Hall in 1642

The later Cordells

Robert Cordell (c.1616–80) re-established the family in Suffolk, serving as MP for Sudbury and Sheriff of the county and being created a baronet in 1660. After the ransacking of 1642, he was faced with repairing the house and refurnishing it from scratch. He seems to have found the task as onerous as the Savages: in his later years he was described as 'a poor gentleman that has almost spent all'. He was succeeded by a son and grandson (both called John and both local MPs), who lived quietly at Melford for the rest of the century. The latter, Sir John Cordell, 3rd Bt, died in 1704 at the age of only 26 after falling from his horse. He had no children, and so left the estate to his sister Margaret.

The Firebraces

In 1710 Margaret Cordell married Charles Firebrace (1680–1727), the son of a wine merchant who had been Chief Clerk of the Kitchen to both Charles I and II. Their eldest son, who was christened Cordell in honour of his mother's family, inherited Melford in 1727 at the age of only thirteen. Not long after he came of age in 1733, he commissioned a detailed survey of the house and grounds which reveals that little had changed since the 1630s. He then set about modernising the house with gusto. Before 1735, he demolished the east range with its central gatehouse, leaving the present U-shaped building. He also removed the bay windows at the east ends of the two remaining wings and put in sash-windows throughout. Inside, he redecorated in delicate Rococo style, with curly new fire-places, ceiling plasterwork and fixed picture frames, in which he set some of the old family portraits. Sadly, much of his best work was in the north wing and was destroyed by the 1942 fire, but you can still see something of the effect in the Blue Drawing Room.

Unlike two previous owners of Melford, Sir Cordell Firebrace was not bankrupted by the cost of redecorating, having in 1737 taken the precaution of marrying Bridget Evers, a widow who came with a fortune of £25,000. But like several of his predecessors, he died childless, in 1759. His widow remarried the aristocratic squire of Lyston Hall, but continued to use the house until her own death in 1782. Four years later, her second husband sold Melford to Sir Harry Parker, 6th Bt. The line established at Melford by Sir William Cordell in the 1540s and maintained over 250 years had finally come to an end.

(Right) Sir Charles Firebrace, 2nd Bt

The Rococo plasterwork decoration of the
Cordell Room was commissioned in the 1730s
by Sir Cordell Firebrace, 3rd Bt.
Most of it was destroyed in
the 1942 fire

Sir Cordell Firebrace,
3rd Bt, and his wife
Bridget

The Parkers
A naval dynasty

Sir Harry Parker, 6th Bt, acquired the estate and the house complete with much of its existing furnishings, including the old portraits enshrined in Sir Cordell Firebrace's drawing room. Sir Harry came from an ancient Devon family that included the Parkers of Saltram near Plymouth (now also a property of the National Trust). It was one of the great naval dynasties. From the Seven Years War in the 1750s until the Second World War, five generations of his relatives fought – and died – at sea for their country. Confusingly for us, several of the more distinguished were christened Hyde, in honour of a famous ancestor, Charles II's Lord Chancellor, Edward Hyde, Earl of Clarendon.

Sir Harry's Father: Vice-Admiral Sir Hyde Parker I, 5th Bt (1713–83)

He began his career as a merchant seaman, joining the Royal Navy at 24 in 1737. Five years later, he was given his first command. Hyde Parker I was lucky to survive Anson's epic voyage round the world in 1744. Following the outbreak of the Seven Years War in 1756, he was sent to the Indian Ocean, where he took part in the capture of Manila from the Spanish.

In 1778 he was promoted rear-admiral and dispatched to the other side of the world to confront the French navy in the Caribbean. Victories in St Lucia and Martinique followed. In 1781 he returned to home waters, where he engaged a Dutch fleet near the Dogger Bank in the North Sea. A fierce battle ensued, which ended inconclusively. Hyde Parker felt that his squadron had not been properly equipped for the assignment and insisted on resigning his command. He had a change of heart the following year, when he was appointed to the East Indies command. In December 1782 he set sail in HMS *Cato* from Rio de Janeiro to take up his post in Bombay on the other side of the Pacific. The *Cato* was never heard of again, and it is now thought that she went down off the Maldives. Among those who were lost with Admiral Hyde Parker was Sir Harry's young son, who was serving with his grandfather as a midshipman.

Brother: Admiral Sir Hyde Parker II (1739–1807)

Having served much of his early naval career in his father's ships, Hyde Parker II made his name fighting in the American War of Independence. In 1776 he managed to break the boom which the American rebels had set up across the

Hudson River near New York. Although the war ended in defeat for the British, Hyde Parker was knighted for his part in the campaign. In 1780 his ship, the *Phoenix*, was wrecked by a hurricane on the coast of hostile Cuba. He and his crew managed to scramble ashore. The prize money he won while serving in the West Indies during the 1790s made him a wealthy man.

In 1801, at the age of 61, he was appointed to command a British fleet which had been ordered to bombard the heavily defended port of Copenhagen. His second-in-command was Horatio Nelson, who led the attack. At the height of the battle, Hyde Parker II hoisted the general sign no. 39, 'Discontinue the action'. Hyde Parker never explained his decision, but it has recently been suggested that he had received news from secret sources of the assassination of the Russian tsar Paul, which made the conflict unnecessary. Whatever the reason, Nelson decided to ignore this direct order, famously raising his telescope to his blind eye and exclaiming, 'I really do not see the signal'.

Sir Hyde Parker II, painted by Romney on the shore of the Hudson River near New York, where he distinguished himself in 1776 during the American War of Independence. In the background is his ship, the Phoenix

Spoils of war

In 1762 Hyde Parker I was commanding HMS *Panther* as part of the British expedition against the Spanish colony of Manila. On 31 October he engaged the *Santissima Trinidad*, a huge Spanish galleon *en route* from Manila to Acapulco with a hold full of gold and precious china. After a two-hour battle, the *Santissima Trinidad* surrendered. Her cargo was valued at £600,000, and as the victorious captain, Hyde Parker was entitled to £10,000. Although Hyde Parker did not live to see Melford, much of his prize booty found its way here, including the superb Chinese vases on the staircase and in the Library.

Nelson pressed on with the action, ultimately compelling the Danish forces to capitulate.

Nephew: Vice-Admiral Hyde Parker III (1786–1854)

Hyde Parker III also served in the Napoleonic Wars and rose to the top of his profession, becoming Senior Naval Lord in 1852. His son, yet another Hyde Parker (1824–54), commanded the first steamship in the Royal Navy, HMS *Firebrand*, and was killed storming a Russian fort at Sulina in the Crimea in 1854. His grandson, Edmund Hyde Parker (later Admiral), commanded the battleship *Superb* at the Battle of Jutland in 1916.

Sir William Parker, 7th Bt (1769–1830)

The 6th Baronet's son William inherited Melford in 1812 and the following year he commissioned the architect Thomas Hopper to modernise the house, which had once again grown old-fashioned. Hopper respected the mellow 16th-century exterior, but was more radical inside.

On the ground floor of the west range, Hopper ingeniously enclosed an outside loggia and removed the central staircase next to it to create a new two-room Library for the 7th Baronet's substantial collection of books. The result is an elegant Regency reading room, but the slipshod conversion left a legacy of serious structural problems for the 7th Baronet's successors to resolve. At the same time, Hopper inserted an impressive processional staircase at the south end of the Hall, which he recast, adding a new roof and ceiling above. He also installed central heating in the principal ground-floor rooms, which was then still a very new idea. Although the 7th Baronet was a bachelor, he needed more bedrooms for visiting relatives, which Hopper provided. The work was completed in 1820, and for the next ten years the 7th Baronet was content to live the quiet life of an unmarried country gentleman, fulfilling his local responsibilities as colonel of the West Suffolk Militia.

Sir Hyde Parker, 8th Bt (1785–1856)

On Sir William Parker's death in 1830, Melford passed to his younger brother, another Hyde and also a bachelor. In 1838 the 8th Baronet asked a neighbour and amateur architect, Col. Rushbrooke, to design a new entrance lodge with little turrets modelled on those of the house. He also recalled Thomas Hopper in 1840 to carry out extensive further work on the north wing. This entailed designing a double-height drawing room and a saloon with a large bay window (destroyed in 1942 and not

Melford Hall in 1818

replaced). Despite all his work on Melford, the 8th Baronet lived abroad for long periods, enjoying cruises in his private yacht between his properties in Sardinia and Sweden, where he pioneered the sport of fly-fishing. He died in 1856, and once again the estate went sideways – to a nephew, William Parker.

Sir William Parker, 9th Bt (1826–91)

The 9th Baronet was a younger son, who inherited the baronetcy and the estate only because his elder brother had been killed fighting in the Crimean War. He also inherited alarming debts and so was obliged to let out the house and estate for shooting. During this period, he lived at Bridge House in the village, where his thirteen children were born. He was fascinated by Melford and was to become the family historian, writing scholarly accounts of the village and of the Parkers. The 9th Baronet's antiquarian tastes encouraged him to refurnish the older rooms such as the Hall with Jacobean panelling and dark oak antiques. He also restored this room's traditional mullioned windows in 1867. At the same time, he devoted his considerable abilities to improving the estate. His motto was 'Never trust agents; do it yourself'.

The Rev. Sir William Hyde Parker, 10th Bt (1863–1931)

The 10th Baronet was Sir William's second son, and, like many younger sons, took Holy Orders, becoming a chaplain to the Bishop of Barbados. But he was obliged to return to Britain on the death of his elder brother in 1887. Although he became the 10th Baronet in 1891, he continued to serve the parish as the Rev. Sir William Hyde Parker, preaching in Long Melford church in a Suffolk dialect. One of the last squarson masters of foxhounds, he often appeared with his riding boots showing beneath his cassock. In 1890 he had married Ethel Leech, a cousin of Beatrix Potter, who often visited Melford in the following years and tried out her famous stories on the Hyde Parker children.

The antiquarian Sir William Parker, 9th Bt, who was painted, appropriately, in the Library at Melford. The book he is shown reading features a view of Melford Hall and its banqueting house

The parson squire Sir William Hyde Parker, 10th Bt

41

Sir William Hyde Parker, 11th Bt (1892–1951)

The 10th Baronet died in February 1931. The following November, his son and heir Willy married Ulla Ditlef-Nielsen, who had been brought up in a very different world in Denmark and had little time to adjust. As there were death-duties to be paid, the sizeable staff had to be cut back. The 11th Baronet also began farming much of the estate himself, because tenants were hard to find during the agricultural depression of the 1930s. Inside the house, the Hyde Parkers modernised the services, introducing electric light in the Great Saloon, drawing room and dining room, but the Hall continued to be lit by gas, the kitchen and bedrooms by candles and gas.

Lady Hyde Parker rescued the Regency library furniture, which a previous generation had banished to the attics. She was also keen to get rid of the lingering Victorian décor of terracotta and olive green: 'I've always been interested in interior colouring. I always longed

Sir William Hyde Parker, 11th Bt

to have Melford painted in pale colours. Because in Denmark we have to spend so much time in our homes in the winter, I think on the whole I feel more conscious of them and how they are arranged. We have a lot of light colours. When I did up the Victorian bedrooms here, I put white curtains under the muslin.'

The Second World War was to present the house and the Hyde Parkers with challenges of an altogether greater order.

The Fire

Following the outbreak of war in 1939, Melford Hall was requisitioned by the army. The house became the officers' mess for a succession of army regiments, while the park was filled with Nissen huts. On the evening of 21 February 1942 the Hyde Parkers were invited to a dance in the house in aid of War Weapons Week. Unfortunately, a fire broke out in a sealed room in the north wing, which smouldered during the night and spread. The fire was not detected until the following morning, by which time the north wing was well alight. The blaze gutted the north wing and destroyed the roof of the west range. The best of the surviving Rococo decoration, much fine furniture and many large paintings were also lost.

This was the second such disaster to strike the family: their London home had received a direct hit during the Blitz of 1941.

Reconstruction

The Hyde Parkers could have been forgiven for giving up Melford at this point. But Lady Hyde Parker was adamant, as she remembered years later:

It never struck me that I wasn't to carry on. I suppose I saw the difficulties, because I had had enough warning: "What are you going to do? You can't possibly live in that great big place", people would say. "But why not?" "You can't possibly move back. I know the family won't blame you." My reply was "Well, Willy would have gone back to Melford." … I knew how he loved the place; a house like this is not just bricks and mortar, it's more personal, something which has been going on for generations. Willy wouldn't have let it down. I couldn't let it down either.

The Hyde Parkers turned to Prof. Sir Albert Richardson, an architect with a love of old buildings and much experience of restoring them from the ravages of war. Despite the severe restrictions on building materials, he was able to rebuild the gutted north wing in its original external form; but, in the long tradition of Melford architects, he was more radical inside. Concrete beams were inserted to support the new floors, and a new suite of family rooms was created in the north wing incorporating an old staircase from Cambridge. Here Lady Hyde Parker had a chance to apply her tastes with brilliant results. The floors were laid with pale polished stone slabs, and the walls were painted white. Pale fabrics were chosen for the sofas and curtains, and the tables given glass tops – all to produce the sense of Scandinavian light and transparency that Lady Hyde Parker remembered from her youth. As more and more old country houses are being repainted in their 'correct' Victorian colours, the post-war redecoration of Melford is becoming increasingly rare and interesting.

The National Trust

On the death of the 11th Baronet in 1951, his widow faced death-duties set at 50 per cent of land-related assets and 80 per cent of all other assets. She was determined to retain land, as the family had started to farm the estate after the First World War. So the ancient woodland

was clear-felled and leased to the Forestry Commission, which planted pine. Against all advice, Lady Hyde Parker clung on to the estate, eventually settling a large proportion of the remaining tax bill by transferring the house, some of the principal contents and 130 acres of the park to the Treasury. In 1960 they were passed to the National Trust so that they might be preserved for everyone's enjoyment. Lady Hyde Parker opened the house to the public, and having demonstrated its viability, agreed to continue opening for the National Trust.

In the 1970s Sir Richard Hyde Parker, 12th Bt, and his wife Jeanie made their home in the south wing after restoring an interior little changed since the army had left in 1945. They continue to live at Melford with their family.

Ulla, Lady Hyde Parker in 1934, three years after she married Sir William Hyde Parker. Together, they repaired the house after the fire and redecorated their quarters in a distinctive Scandinavian style

The Hyde Parkers of Melford

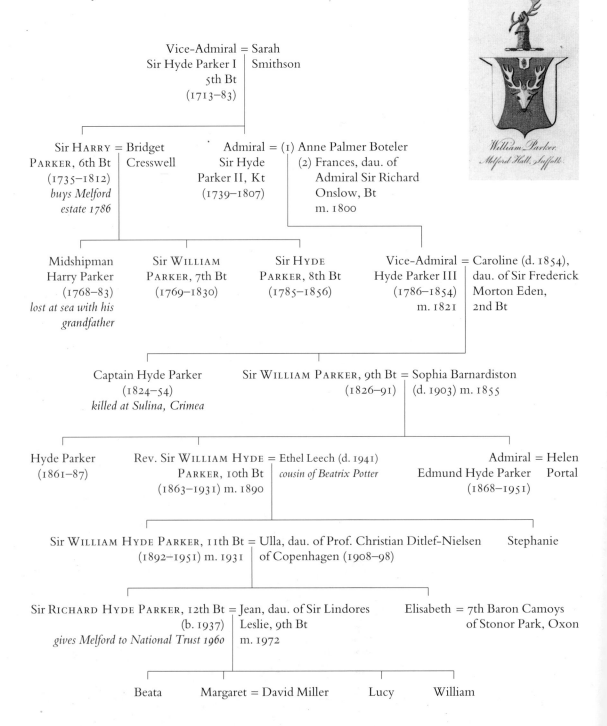

Vice-Admiral = Sarah
Sir Hyde Parker I | Smithson
5th Bt
(1713–83)

Sir HARRY = Bridget
PARKER, 6th Bt | Cresswell
(1735–1812)
*buys Melford
estate 1786*

Admiral = (1) Anne Palmer Boteler
Sir Hyde | (2) Frances, dau. of
Parker II, Kt | Admiral Sir Richard
(1739–1807) | Onslow, Bt
| m. 1800

Midshipman
Harry Parker
(1768–83)
*lost at sea with his
grandfather*

Sir WILLIAM
PARKER, 7th Bt
(1769–1830)

Sir HYDE
PARKER, 8th Bt
(1785–1856)

Vice-Admiral = Caroline (d. 1854),
Hyde Parker III | dau. of Sir Frederick
(1786–1854) | Morton Eden,
m. 1821 | 2nd Bt

Captain Hyde Parker
(1824–54)
killed at Sulina, Crimea

Sir WILLIAM PARKER, 9th Bt = Sophia Barnardiston
(1826–91) | (d. 1903) m. 1855

Hyde Parker
(1861–87)

Rev. Sir WILLIAM HYDE = Ethel Leech (d. 1941)
PARKER, 10th Bt | *cousin of Beatrix Potter*
(1863–1931) m. 1890

Admiral = Helen
Edmund Hyde Parker | Portal
(1868–1951)

Sir WILLIAM HYDE PARKER, 11th Bt = Ulla, dau. of Prof. Christian Ditlef-Nielsen
(1892–1951) m. 1931 | of Copenhagen (1908–98)

Stephanie

Sir RICHARD HYDE PARKER, 12th Bt = Jean, dau. of Sir Lindores
(b. 1937) | Leslie, 9th Bt
gives Melford to National Trust 1960 | m. 1972

Elisabeth = 7th Baron Camoys
of Stonor Park, Oxon

Beata   Margaret = David Miller   Lucy   William